THE
7 HIDDEN TRAPS
THAT SINK
BOOK LAUNCHES

A Strategic Guide to Book Marketing, Audience
Building, and Turning Your Book into a Platform

KEREN KILGORE

THE 7 HIDDEN TRAPS THAT SINK BOOK LAUNCHES

A Strategic Guide to Book Marketing, Audience Building, and Turning Your Book into a Platform

KEREN KILGORE

PORT ST. LUCIE, FLORIDA

Cover and Interior Design by Quantum Shift Media

ISBN: 978-1-955533-52-2 (print)
ISBN: 978-1-955533-53-9 (eBook)

Library of Congress Control Number: 2026907103

Printed in the United States

PORT ST. LUCIE, FLORIDA

DEDICATION

To my favorite husband, Michael. You believed in me when I doubted myself, supported every vision I had, even the crazy ones, and stood beside me through every season of our lives. Your steadiness, encouragement, and love have carried me farther than I ever could have gone alone. You are, and always have been, the wind beneath my wings.

CONTENTS

FOREWORD

For the past 30 years, I've been helping authors turn mediocre books into great books. When I was in my twenties, I worked for a nonprofit publishing company, and part of my job was to read manuscripts before they were published.

On my very first assignment, I saw that something essential was missing. The content was thoughtful. The ideas were solid. But the application for the reader wasn't clear. It lacked movement.

As I read, I found myself thinking,

If this were rephrased....

If different questions were asked....

If this idea were drawn out more clearly...the reader would experience a shift.

When I suggested those changes and watched the piece come to life, something clicked. I realized I had a gift for making books better. I could see not just what the author was saying, but also what the reader needed to be transformed by it.

For years, that became my focus—strengthening manuscripts, clarifying ideas, helping authors articulate their message in a way that truly landed. I loved the craft of it. I loved watching a paragraph sharpen into clarity, and an idea expand into impact.

But over time, I began to notice something else. A beautifully written book did not automatically become an influential one. Some authors produced excellent work, and it quietly disappeared. Others, sometimes with less polished prose, experienced tremendous momentum. Their books opened doors. Elevated their authority. Attracted opportunities. That contrast forced me to look deeper.

That's when I understood the second layer of my work. Improving the manuscript was only the beginning. What truly lit me up was watching a book activate something in its author—watching it raise their credibility, open stages, attract aligned clients, and create leverage inside their business. I wasn't just refining sentences anymore. I was also helping architect platforms.

So my work expanded. I began guiding authors not only in strengthening their message but also in positioning it. Through clarifying how their book fits inside their business. Through mapping how it could open opportunities, generate revenue pathways, and build long-term authority. We would talk about audience, integration, speaking strategy, lead magnets, launch structure, and momentum—not as afterthoughts, but as part of the design.

Because a manuscript alone is potential, but a strategically positioned book is powerful.

A book can sit quietly on a shelf, or it can become an authoritative asset that grows a business, deepens impact, and multiplies opportunity. The difference is not talent. It's not luck. It's not hustle.

It is intention, integration, and strategy.

Every meaningful book begins with a purpose, but not every influential book is positioned with clarity. And that positioning—the integration of message, market, and momentum—is what turns a manuscript into movement.

And here's the part most business owners who author a book don't realize: The integration of message, market, and creation of momentum is also the exact reason a book grows a business. It doesn't grow your business because you put "author" in your bio.

Building Trust at Scale

Most books don't fail because they're poorly written. They fail because they never build trust with enough people.

A book grows your business by creating trust at scale and clarifying your message. It teaches your audience how to think differently. And when it's done well, it naturally opens the door to the next conversation with the reader—whether that's joining your email list, booking a call, attending a workshop, hiring you, or stepping into a deeper transformation.

> **A strategically positioned book can become an authority asset that grows a business, deepens impact, and multiplies opportunity.**

In most businesses, trust is built slowly. It develops through conversations, meetings, referrals, and time spent working with someone. Each interaction helps a potential client or partner decide whether they believe in your expertise and whether they feel confident working with you.

This traditional process builds trust one relationship at a time.

A book changes that dynamic.

When someone reads your book, they spend hours with your ideas, your thinking, and your perspective. They begin to understand how you approach problems, how you guide people through challenges, and what you believe matters most. Long before they ever meet you, they often feel as though they already know you.

This is what I mean by trust at scale.

Instead of explaining your expertise in dozens of individual conversations, your book demonstrates it to hundreds—or even thousands—of readers at the same time. Each reader experiences a form of relationship with you through your words. They see your knowledge in action, your philosophy clearly expressed, and your ability to guide them toward results.

By the time a reader reaches out—whether for coaching, consulting, speaking, or collaboration—they often arrive already aligned with your thinking. Many of their questions have already been answered. They understand how you work and why your approach is valuable.

In many cases, the book has already done the work of building trust.

In that sense, a book becomes far more than content. It becomes a trust-building engine that continues working in the background of your business. While you are serving clients, developing new ideas, or speaking on stages, your book is still out in the world—introducing you, demonstrating your expertise, and building trust with the next person who picks it up.

Over the years, I've worked on every kind of book—college textbooks, novels, memoirs, self-help, business, spiritual, young adult, children's, and everything in between. And I've watched the same pattern repeat itself again and again: a book can be beautifully written and still fail to generate momentum.

And a book can be simple—even imperfect—and become a powerful engine for visibility, connection, and revenue because it's strategically designed to move the reader.

This book you're reading is here to do exactly that: help you generate visibility and income. Because the truth is this: your book isn't just a product—it's a platform.

It's an authority platform that positions your thinking, expertise, and lived experience in a way that extends beyond you. That platform becomes a portal into your message, your mission, and the work you're here to do in the world.

When someone reads your book, they are stepping through that portal. They are entering your worldview. They are beginning a relationship with your ideas. When your book is strategically positioned, they are also stepping into a pathway— into your speaking, services, programs, and leadership.

And if you've written a book—or you're close to finishing one—you've already done something brave. You made something out of nothing. You gave language to what you've lived, what you've learned, and what you know.

Now we're going to make sure it reaches the people it was written for and supports the business you're building.

Unfortunately, many book launches fail to create this kind of trust—not because the book lacks value, but because the author unknowingly falls into a set of hidden traps that quietly undermine the launch before momentum ever begins.

HOW TO USE THIS BOOK

The 7 Hidden Traps is not a book you simply read. It's a book you work with.

If you're holding this in your hands, you likely fall into one of three categories:

1. Your book is written, but you haven't launched it.
2. You launched it once, and it didn't have the impact you hoped for.
3. You are writing it now and want to do it right from the beginning.

Wherever you are, this book is designed to meet you there and move you forward.

You can read it straight through from beginning to end. That will give you the full framework—the mindset, the strategy, and the structure needed to turn your book into a growth engine for your business.

Or you can use it diagnostically.

Each of the seven traps stands on its own. As you read, you may recognize yourself immediately in one of them. When that happens, slow down. That's your leverage point. That's where your growth is waiting.

You don't need to fix all seven traps at once.

You need to identify the one that is currently costing you the most—in visibility, in revenue, or in momentum—and begin there.

This book is built around the same strategic framework I teach inside the 7 Hidden Traps That Sink Book Launches Masterclass. The traps you'll encounter are not theoretical—they correspond to real breakdown points I've seen over three decades of publishing and launching books.

And each trap has a structured solution that can be used to get out of or avoid altogether.

90-Day Book Launch Blueprint

To learn more about the 90-Day Book Launch Blueprint, click the QR Code or visit 90-Day Book Launch Blueprint.

The Blueprint provides the implementation system—the customized timeline, marketing sequence, monetization pathway, and post-launch strategy.

This book gives you the clarity to understand where you're stuck. The Blueprint gives you the path to move forward.

If you already have access to the Blueprint, use this book as your strategic companion. Let it deepen your understanding and sharpen your execution.

If you don't have access to the Blueprint, this book will still guide you in avoiding the traps and finding the solutions to a cohesive launch plan.

You may notice that I repeat a few core principles throughout this book. That's intentional. Launching a book that grows your business is less about collecting more tactics and more about committing to a clear structure and staying with it.

Momentum matters more than perfection.

Clarity matters more than complexity.

Connection matters more than cleverness.

Structure matters more than inspiration alone.

And most of all, your book matters.

As you move through these pages, keep one question in front of you: How can your book become a platform into the work you are truly here to do? If you let that question guide you, the strategies that follow will begin to organize themselves around your purpose. Your book is not meant to sit quietly on a shelf. It is meant to move readers, conversations, and your business forward.

Quick Assessment

Before we go any further, take a moment and answer this question honestly. When it comes to launching (or preparing to launch) your book, which of the following feels most true right now?

- I feel overwhelmed by all the marketing advice out there.
- I don't know where to start.
- I don't have a clear strategy.
- I'm unsure how this book will actually grow my business.
- I don't have a mailing list or platform.
- I struggle with tech or marketing execution.
- I feel alone in the process and second-guess my decisions.
- I launched once and lost momentum.
- I'm afraid it won't work.

Note the one that makes your stomach tighten a little. That's your starting point.

Most authors believe their struggle is personal—a lack of discipline, confidence, or knowledge. It's not.

In 30 years of publishing and launching books, I've seen the same seven patterns surface again and again. They are predictable. They are common. And most importantly, they are fixable. This book will walk you through each one.

But before we do, I want you to reconnect with something more important than strategy. Because your launch is not just a marketing event. It is the fulfillment of a promise.

THREE BIRTHS AND
A SOUL AGREEMENT

At some point—before there was a manuscript, before there was a table of contents, before there was even a title—there was a knowing. A quiet (or not so quiet) awareness that something inside you needed to be written.

Maybe it was a story you lived.

Maybe it was a framework you developed.

Maybe it was years of experience your clients kept thanking you for.

Maybe it was pure entertainment—something joyful that wanted to exist in the world.

Whatever form it took, you didn't write your book by accident. You wrote it because you believed it could make a difference.

That belief matters.

In more than 30 years in publishing, I've had thousands of conversations with authors and read countless manuscripts. I've worked with writers across every category—business owners, novelists, memoirists, educators, speakers, coaches, and storytellers of every kind.

And no matter the genre, every meaningful book begins with the same starting point:

Purpose.

When you decided to write your book, you made a kind of agreement with your reader. A quiet agreement that says: If you trust me with your time, I will offer you something valuable. I will help you see differently. I will move you forward in some way.

That agreement begins the moment you start writing.

But something many authors don't realize is this: A book is not born once. It is born three times: when it is written, when it is published, and when it finds its readers.

The first birth is writing—when the ideas, story, or message come into existence.

The second birth is publishing—when the manuscript becomes a real book that can enter the world.

And the third birth is marketing—when the book begins finding the readers it was written for.

Many authors celebrate the first birth and work hard to achieve the second. But it is the third birth that determines whether the book will actually fulfill its purpose.

Writing your book brings it into existence.

Publishing your book makes it available.

Marketing your book is what allows it to make an impact.

If your book is meant to grow your business, then marketing it strategically is not self-promotion—it is stewardship.

Because a successful book launch is not about ego. It is about reach. It is about relationships.

And it is about revenue pathways that allow you to continue serving.

The Soul Agreement

There is something else I've noticed over the years. Books have a way of choosing their authors.

You may have decided to write your book. And in one sense, you did. But if you're honest, there was also a pull. A persistence. An idea that would not leave you alone.

I often tell my authors: your book wants to come through you. When you allow that—when you stop forcing and begin listening—something shifts. The book begins to take you on a journey. You follow threads you didn't expect. You refine ideas you thought were settled. You discover clarity you didn't know you were missing.

You are not just writing the book. You are being shaped by it. And in that process, you make a deeper agreement, not merely with your audience, but with the book itself.

It is an agreement to state the concepts accurately. To represent the ideas responsibly. To birth it consciously. Because when a book carries insight that can change lives—or shift thinking—it deserves integrity in its delivery. Meaningful books elevate awareness. They expand understanding. They contribute, in their own way, to raising the consciousness of the planet.

That is not dramatic; it is responsibility. And here is the part many authors miss: The soul agreement is not fulfilled at "The End." It is fulfilled when your message is positioned to travel.

If the book wants to come through you, it also wants to reach the people it was written for.

A book unfinished is incomplete. A book unlaunched is unheard. A book launched without a strategy is underutilized.

Honoring your book means giving it all three births: The birth of being well written; the birth of being in print, and the birth of reaching its readers.

Pause here and ask yourself:

What soul agreement does your book ask of you?
Does it ask you to be clearer?
More specific?
More courageous?
More disciplined in finishing?
More intentional in launching?

Write it down.

Because your clarity about this agreement will shape how you steward these births. If you have launched before and felt disappointed, you did not fail. You gathered data. I do not believe in failure; I believe in correct and continue.

If visibility was low, that's data. If monetization wasn't clear, that's data. If momentum faded, that's data. Data can be corrected. And corrected action creates new results.

This book exists so you can clearly see where the breakdown happened—or where it might happen—and address it before it costs you time, energy, and confidence because your book deserves your commitment.

Before we move into the lessons of the seven traps, pause for a moment and answer these two questions:

Who is your book meant to help?
And what do you want to change for them?

Be specific and take notes. The clarity of your answer will determine:

- Your launch messaging
- Your platform focus
- Your lead magnet
- Your speaking strategy
- Your revenue pathway

Your book is not random. It is targeted.

And when you align your launch with that clarity, everything becomes simpler.

In the chapters ahead, we will walk through the seven hidden traps that quietly sink book launches. Some are tactical. Some are structural. Some are psychological. All of them are solvable. And as we solve them, we are not just building a better launch.

We are honoring the agreement your book made with you and the business you are building around it. Because writing a powerful book builds the platform. Launching it strategically activates it.

THE LAUNCH REALITY CHECK

What Most People Get Wrong

If you've ever felt overwhelmed at the thought of launching your book, you are not alone.

If you've ever opened your laptop, searched "how to launch a book," and felt your nervous system tighten within minutes, you are not alone.

Most book launches do not fail for lack of talent.

They fail because of a lack of structure.

Before we walk through the seven hidden traps, we need to clear away a few common myths, because these myths quietly sabotage otherwise brilliant books.

Analysis Paralysis

One of the most common mistakes authors make is chasing tactics. You hear that you need a launch team or that you need paid ads. Someone says you must be on TikTok. Someone else insists you need a podcast tour. Another expert says you need 100 reviews in week one.

So you try something. Maybe two things. Maybe five.

You post consistently for a couple of weeks. You send an email to your list. You consider running ads but hesitate. You're thinking about pitching podcasts but aren't sure how to get started.

And then something subtle happens. You stall. Not because you lack motivation. Not because you lack intelligence. But because you are overloaded. Too many options create analysis paralysis. When every tactic feels urgent, none of them feel clear. Without a defined sequence—without knowing what comes first, what comes next, and what actually matters—every action competes for your attention.

Random tactics fail because they are disconnected from a system.

A successful launch is not a collection of marketing tricks; it is a structured progression.

The Myths That Quietly Sabotage Authors

There are two myths that keep authors stuck longer than almost anything else.

The first myth is that visibility must come before the launch.

Many business owners tell themselves they will launch once they have a larger audience. Once their email list grows. Once their social media following feels substantial enough.

This belief keeps books unpublished and launches delayed for months—sometimes years.

The truth is that visibility grows through the launch, not before it.

A strategic launch gives you a reason to reach out, collaborate, speak, pitch podcasts, invite endorsements, and re-engage your network. The launch itself becomes the engine that expands your visibility.

Waiting for visibility before launching is like waiting to get in shape before going to the gym.

The second myth is quieter but just as powerful: the belief that book sales alone will create wealth.

Somewhere beneath the surface, many authors imagine that once the book is released, sales will generate ongoing income. They picture bestseller status or steady royalties.

When that doesn't happen immediately, discouragement sets in.

Book sales alone rarely build significant wealth.

Revenue comes from what the book activates—speaking engagements, consulting contracts, coaching programs, partnerships, and expanded opportunities. The book is not the primary revenue source.

It is the platform that opens revenue pathways.

When this distinction becomes clear, disappointment is replaced by strategy.

The Truth: A Launch Is a System and a Relationship Plan

A launch is not hype.

It is not intensity.

It is not one big week of activity.

A successful launch is two things: A system and a relationship plan.

The system provides structure—a timeline, messaging sequence, visibility strategy, monetization pathway, and post-launch plan. Structure removes guesswork and reduces overwhelm.

The relationship plan builds trust—with your launch team, your email list, podcast hosts, event organizers, collaborators, and readers. Without relationships, even the best system feels mechanical. Without structure, even strong relationships feel scattered.

Both are essential.

When structure and relationship work together, launches feel grounded instead of frantic. Intentional instead of reactive.

And when you begin to see your launch this way, rather than a burst of marketing activity, but as a strategic system designed to strengthen relationships—everything changes.

Next, we'll begin identifying the seven hidden traps that quietly undermine that system and how to correct them. Because once you understand the traps, you stop internalizing the struggle. You begin correcting it.

TRAP 1

"I DON'T KNOW WHERE TO START"

There is a very specific kind of frustration that comes with launching a book.

You've done the hard part. You wrote it. You revised it. You refined it. You carried the idea from knowing to a manuscript. You may even be holding the printed copy in your hands.

And then you sit down to launch it.

You open your laptop, type a few notes, and suddenly the clarity you had while writing disappears.

Should you build a launch team first?

Should you begin posting consistently on social media?

Should you pitch podcasts?

Should you create a lead magnet?

Should you redesign your website?

Should you run ads?

Within minutes, your mind is crowded with options.

And when there are too many options, there is no obvious starting point.

So you delay.

Not because you don't care. Not because you lack discipline. But because you genuinely don't know which step matters most.

That feeling—that quiet, paralyzing confusion—is the first trap.

What This Trap Feels Like

It feels like overwhelm. It feels like staring at too many open browser tabs. It feels like knowing your book has value but not knowing how to move it forward without wasting time or energy.

Sometimes it even feels embarrassing. You may have built a business. You may have led teams. You may be highly competent in your field. And yet here you are, frozen in front of your own launch.

Weeks pass. You tell yourself you're "researching." You watch webinars. You download checklists. You consider strategies.

What's really happening is not confusion. It's the absence of sequence.

When you don't have a defined launch timeline, your brain cannot prioritize. Every task feels equally important. Without structure, the mind defaults to avoidance, not because it's lazy, but because it's overloaded.

Launching a book without a clear framework is like building a house without architectural plans. You may have all the materials—the manuscript, the cover, the website, the contacts—but you don't know what to assemble first. So nothing gets assembled.

The Hidden Cost: Doubt and Delays

The hidden cost of this trap is rarely dramatic at first. It doesn't look like failure. It looks like delay.

A week passes. Then two. Then a month.

Momentum fades. Excitement cools. Doubt creeps in quietly. You begin to question whether the launch will matter as much as you once believed.

There is also a financial cost. Every week the book sits idle is a week it is not building visibility, not strengthening trust, not opening revenue pathways inside your business. Momentum compounds. So does hesitation.

Case Studies

I worked with with Kathy Ziola on her book *Live Compassion*, a 365-day meditation rooted in nonviolent communication. The book was thoughtful and beautifully written. But when it came time to launch, she felt completely stuck. She had ideas, but no sequence. Every option felt overwhelming.

Once she began working from a structured timeline, the energy changed. She printed it out and kept it beside her computer. Each day, she focused only on the task in front of her. Instead of asking, "What should I be doing?" she asked, "What is next?"

The mental load decreased. The momentum increased.

She successfully launched the book, and later used the same structure to launch it again. The difference was not effort; it was order.

Karen Krueger, a novelist, didn't struggle with ideas—she had a powerful, emotionally layered story in *Arrested Love*. She knew the depth of what she had written. But when it came time to begin the launch process, she found herself stuck in a different way: I don't know where to start.

There were so many possible directions. Build an audience. Create content. Reach out for reviews. Each piece felt important, but without a clear starting point, everything blurred together. The weight of all the "shoulds" made it hard to take the first step.

Once Karen stepped into the structured process of the Blueprint, that changed.

Instead of trying to do everything at once, she focused on what came first—and only that. One step led to the next. The noise quieted. The path became visible. What had felt overwhelming became actionable.

Karen didn't need more ideas. She needed a place to begin. And once she had it, momentum followed.

The Fix: A Proven Pathway

The solution to this trap is not more information. It is not another checklist. It is not a new tactic. It is a structure. When you do not know where to start, what you are actually missing is a starting line.

The overwhelm does not come from a lack of motivation. It comes from a lack of sequence. When everything feels important, nothing feels actionable. And when nothing feels actionable, momentum stalls.

You do not need to invent the roadmap while standing inside the launch. You need a proven pathway.

This is exactly why the 90-Day Book Launch Blueprint was created. It removes the burden of designing the sequence yourself. Instead of carrying the entire launch in your head, you are guided step by step inside a structured timeline that tells you what matters now and what can wait.

You stop asking, "What should I be doing?"

You start knowing, "This is what I'm doing this week."

That shift alone reduces mental noise dramatically.

Clarity restores calm. Calm restores action. Action restores momentum.

When the structure exists outside you, you are free to focus on execution rather than constant decision-making. And that is how this first trap loses its power.

Books rarely fail loudly. They stall quietly. And stalling almost always begins with not knowing where to start.

In the next chapter, we'll explore the second trap—overwhelm from too many marketing options—and why trying to do everything almost guarantees you'll finish nothing.

"I'M OVERWHELMED WITH MARKETING"

If Trap #1 feels like not knowing where to begin, Trap #2 feels like trying to begin everywhere at once.

This is the trap of conflicting advice. You join a Facebook group, and someone insists you need paid ads. You attend a webinar and hear that ads are a waste of money. One expert says TikTok is everything. Another says podcasts are the real play. Someone else says build a launch team of 200 people. Another says you only need 20 superfans.

So you try one thing.

You post consistently for two weeks.

It doesn't explode.

You try something else.

You pitch a few podcasts.

You don't hear back right away.

You get tired. And you stop.

It isn't that you aren't capable. It's that you are stretched thin. And stretched thin rarely produces traction.

What This Trap Feels Like

This trap feels like noise. It feels like trying to drink from a firehose. It feels like working hard without clear results.

You may even feel behind. You look at other authors and think they must know something you don't. You assume they have access to a secret tactic you're missing.

The truth is far simpler: They chose, and you haven't yet. The root cause of this trap is not a lack of discipline; it's too many options.

Modern marketing offers more channels than ever before. Social media platforms, paid ads, email marketing, podcast tours, webinars, live events, collaborations, affiliate campaigns, book clubs, LinkedIn outreach, direct mail, and more.

Every single one of these can work. That is precisely the problem. When everything works, nothing is prioritized. Your brain defaults to experimentation instead of execution.

You keep learning. You keep researching. You keep consuming strategy content. But implementation stays shallow. This is the hidden loop: learning feels productive, but without depth in any one channel, momentum never compounds.

The Hidden Cost: Consistent Visibility

The cost of this trap is not obvious at first. It feels like effort, but it produces fatigue. You spend time learning new platforms. You tweak messaging constantly. You pivot before traction has time to build. The result is fragmented energy. And fragmented energy rarely produces results.

There is also a confidence cost. When you try something briefly and it doesn't produce immediate results, you internalize it as failure. Not because the channel didn't work—but because it was never given enough time or focus to mature.

This trap costs you consistency. And consistency is where visibility compounds.

Case Study

Alana wrote *The Art of Feminine Seduction*, a relationship book rooted in her lived experience navigating the dating world. When she began planning her launch, she was exposed to the same noise most authors face.

She could have tried everything. Instead, she chose two channels: social media and speaking engagements. She committed to consistent, intentional posting that aligned with her audience. And she actively pursued speaking opportunities where her message would resonate.

She did not chase ads. She did not focus on literary awards. She focused on social media and speaking. That focus allowed her messaging to build momentum. Her audience grew steadily. Her visibility deepened. And she became a number-one bestselling author in multiple categories, competing alongside far more established names.

The difference was not volume. It was clarity.

The Fix: A Structured Focus

The antidote to overwhelm is not more exposure. It is focus.

When you try to show up everywhere, you dilute your energy everywhere. When you attempt five visibility channels at once, it is difficult for any of them to gain depth. And without depth, trust does not form.

For any given launch, you do not need to be omnipresent. You need concentration.

The shift happens when you stop asking, "Where should I be?" and start asking, "Where will I go deep?"

Focus consolidates energy. Repetition builds recognition. Recognition builds trust.

But choosing wisely is not as simple as picking two platforms at random. It requires alignment—alignment with your strengths, your network, your message, and your business goals.

This is where structure matters again.

Inside the 90-Day Book Launch Blueprint, visibility is not treated as a buffet of marketing ideas. It is curated. The framework walks you through intentionally selecting your primary channels and strategically sequencing them. Instead of scattering your efforts, you deepen them. Instead of chasing trends, you build traction.

And this is not something you do alone.

As part of the Blueprint, you receive a private strategy session with me. In that session, we design a focused launch plan for your book and your business. We look at your strengths, existing audience, goals, and offers. Together, we determine which marketing strategies make sense for this launch—and which ones can wait.

That conversation alone often eliminates months of guesswork.

The Blueprint makes you deliberate. It narrows your options into a focused plan for this specific launch—while preserving other strategies for future relaunches.

Overwhelm fades when decision-making becomes structured. And structured focus restores momentum.

Next, we'll examine Trap #3—the difficulty of turning a book into a business and why some authors generate attention but fail to convert that attention into revenue.

"I THOUGHT THIS WOULD LEAD TO MORE"

There is a very specific kind of disappointment that comes after a book launch. It doesn't happen immediately. In fact, the launch itself may feel successful. You get congratulations. You receive positive reviews. You may even hit a category ranking. Friends and colleagues celebrate you.

And then, quietly, you wait. You expect the inquiries to increase. You expect the calendar to fill. You expect the opportunities to appear.

And they don't.

Or they don't appear at the level you imagined.

Trap #3 is struggling with how to use your book in your business.

What This Trap Feels Like

It feels confusing.

You wrote a strong book. You launched it. People liked it. So why isn't it translating into business growth?

You may start questioning whether the book was strategic enough. Whether your audience is wrong. Whether your market is too small.

Sometimes it feels like this unspoken thought: *I thought this would lead to more.* More clients. More speaking engagements. More income.

Instead, the book sits in a strange middle ground—respected, but underutilized. The disappointment isn't loud. It's subtle. And subtle disappointment can erode confidence over time.

The Hidden Cost: Missed Opportunities

The hidden cost of this trap is not just financial—though that certainly matters.

It is an opportunity cost.

When a book launches without a defined revenue plan, it becomes a respected artifact instead of a strategic asset.

You may receive praise.

You may gain credibility. You may even see temporary spikes in visibility. But visibility without structure does not automatically convert into revenue. You receive congratulations but not inquiries. You experience attention but not appointments. Your book circulates—but your client pipeline does not expand.

Without a defined monetization pathway, you cannot clearly measure success. You cannot track conversion. You cannot identify breakdowns. You simply feel that something didn't "take off."

There is also a focus cost. When revenue is not intentionally mapped, you default back to your existing marketing habits.

You continue to promote, post, and network—but the book is not structurally integrated into how you acquire clients. It becomes something you talk about, not something that drives business. Over time, this leads to a dangerous belief: *Books don't really grow businesses.* When in truth, books without architecture don't grow businesses.

Case Study

Al Sarno, a therapist, wrote a book called *Joy on the Same Page*. It was thoughtful, grounded, and deeply aligned with his work as a relationship therapist for over 40 years. But like many authors, he initially viewed it as a standalone publication. And he thought his book was so good it would just sell itself. When we stepped back and asked, "How does this book generate business?" everything shifted.

We mapped out how the book could lead to speaking engagements, workshops, and structured therapy intensives. We forecasted revenue not only from book sales, but from the opportunities the book could unlock. What emerged was a $500,000 strategic sales plan, not from selling hundreds of thousands of copies, but from using the book as the authority anchor that positioned him for higher-level work.

The content didn't change. The positioning did.

The Fix: A Business Ecosystem

The solution to this trap is not more marketing. It is pre-launch clarity.

Before visibility intensifies, you must decide how your book fits into your business model—not conceptually, but structurally.

If you cannot clearly articulate how your book generates value beyond book sales, then the launch is incomplete.

A book does not magically create business growth. It must be intentionally integrated into your ecosystem. That integration may include:

- Speaking opportunities
- Consulting or client acquisition
- Programs or services
- Strategic partnerships

This connection must be designed, not assumed.

Inside the 90-Day Book Launch Blueprint, monetization is not treated as an afterthought. We clarify what the book is designed to lead toward before exposure increases. That structural decision shapes your messaging, your targeting, and how you define success.

Inside the Blueprint, we provide 105 book launch and ecosystem strategies you can choose from when launching your book. We recommend using two or three on your first launch and a few more when you relaunch.

Without integration, even strong launches plateau. With integration, your book becomes a business lever.

So pause and ask yourself one honest question: *What is intentionally designed to happen after someone finishes your book?*

Not what you hope happens. Not what might happen. What is structurally positioned to happen?

If that answer feels vague, that is not a personal failure. It is a design gap.

Hope is not a revenue strategy. Structure is.

If the pathway from reader to opportunity is not visible and intentional, attention may rise—but integration will not.

This is why Trap #3 is so dangerous. It masquerades as success. The book launches. The applause happens. But the architecture underneath is missing.

One of the most powerful forms of integration is authority expansion.

Instead of merely selling a book, you position the book as a doorway into higher-level opportunities. When structured correctly, your book supports:

- A clear speaking strategy (local chambers, associations, summits)
- A podcast guest positioning plan
- A media bio and angle sheet
- A TEDx positioning roadmap
- A signature talk extracted directly from your content

This is where books turn into:

- Clients
- Consulting
- Courses
- Retreats
- High-ticket offers

And this is precisely why integration must be intentional.

When the authority pathway is clear, visibility multiplies impact rather than simply increasing noise.

In the next chapter, we'll explore Trap #4—the belief that you need to be a marketing or tech expert to succeed—and why that belief quietly stops more authors than any algorithm ever could.

TRAP 4

"I'M NOT GOOD AT MARKETING"

There is a moment in almost every book launch where confidence falters. It doesn't happen when you're writing the manuscript.

It doesn't happen when you're refining your ideas. It happens when someone says the word "tech."

Landing pages. Email sequences. Automations. Launch funnels. Algorithms.

And suddenly, the internal dialogue begins: *I'm brilliant at my work…but I'm not good at this.*

This is Trap #4. If you don't feel like a marketing guru or tech person, you're not alone.

What This Trap Feels Like

It feels like inadequacy. You are competent in your field. Clients trust you. You've built a business. You've led teams. You've solved complex problems. But marketing systems and tech platforms feel like a different language entirely. You may think: *I don't know how to build landing pages.* Or, *I'm not good at social media.*

So you delay. Or you overcomplicate. Or you assume you need to hire an expensive agency before you even begin.

Underneath it all is one belief: *I need to be tech-savvy to launch successfully.* That belief quietly stops more launches than any algorithm ever could.

The root cause of this trap is assumption. You assume that successful authors are tech experts. You assume there is a complex marketing system you must master before you are allowed to succeed. You assume sophistication equals success.

In reality, clarity equals success. The authors who launch well are not necessarily more technical. They are more structured. They use simple systems consistently rather than complex ones sporadically.

Marketing does not require software brilliance. It requires clarity in communication. And communication is something you already know how to do.

The Hidden Cost: Time, Energy, and Momentum

When you believe you lack the technical ability to launch, you either avoid marketing altogether or overbuild. You spend hours researching platforms. You test tools you don't fully understand. You delay action while trying to perfect the infrastructure.

The cost is time, energy, and momentum.

And often, the cost is money—hiring support before you've clarified the strategy.

But the deeper cost is the erosion of confidence. You begin to think the launch problem is you, when in truth, it's unnecessary complexity.

Case Study

Soozy Miller is a career coach based in New York City. She is brilliant at helping professionals reposition themselves and land high-level roles. When it came time to launch her book, she felt intimidated by the marketing side. She did not consider herself tech-savvy. She didn't know how to structure landing pages or launch emails. The entire process felt foreign.

Instead of trying to master everything at once, she used the provided plug-and-play tools. Templates guided her web designer to create a book landing page. Email frameworks shaped her messaging. A clear launch team communication plan replaced guesswork. She didn't need to become a marketing expert. She needed structure.

The result? A successful launch, multiple bestseller categories, and an award-winning book, not because she became technical overnight, but because she implemented a simple system consistently.

The sophistication wasn't in the tech. It was in the clarity.

The Fix: Plug-and-Play Simplicity

The solution to this trap is not becoming a tech expert. It is reducing the tech to its essentials. Every successful book launch requires only a minimal structure:

- A simple landing page
- A basic email sequence
- A clear communication plan for your launch team
- One or two defined visibility channels

Inside the Blueprint, this is why plug-and-play templates exist. The goal is not to teach you marketing theory. The goal is to remove friction and provide you with landing page templates, email frameworks, launch team scripts, and clear sequences. You do not need to invent. You simply implement them. And that distinction lowers resistance dramatically.

The Blueprint simplifies what feels overwhelming by giving you a minimum viable marketing structure, not an overwhelming one. Simplicity builds momentum. Trap #4 thrives in intimidation. The Blueprint dissolves this in simplicity.

In the next chapter, we'll explore Trap #5—lack of visibility—and why many authors underestimate their ability to build an audience during the launch itself.

TRAP 5

"I DON'T HAVE AN AUDIENCE"

There is a sentence I hear often, sometimes whispered, sometimes stated plainly: "I don't really have a platform." It usually comes with a subtle shrug as if the lack of visibility is an unchangeable condition. As if the launch is already compromised because the audience is too small. Most authors launch with a small list or no list at all.

Trap 5 is the Lack of Visibility and Platform. And it quietly stops more authors than almost anything else.

What This Trap Feels Like

It feels like a disadvantage. You scroll through social media and see authors with tens of thousands of followers. You hear stories about large launch teams and email lists in the tens of thousands. You look at your own numbers and think, *My list is too small. My social media isn't strong. I don't have enough visibility to make this work.*

And so you hesitate. You delay the launch. You tell yourself you'll wait until your audience grows. You assume visibility must precede momentum.

But here's the uncomfortable truth: Waiting for visibility is one of the fastest ways to stay invisible.

The Hidden Cost: No Growth Plan

The root cause of this trap is a false belief: that the platform must come before the launch.

But in reality, visibility often grows through the launch.

A strategic launch gives you a reason to reach out. It gives you a message to share. It creates a focal point for conversations and reactivates dormant relationships. Instead of waiting to "have an audience," you create momentum that builds one.

Most authors underestimate what visibility actually means. They equate audience with social media followers. But audience is not follower count. Audience is access—access to relationships, communities, conversations, and trust.

And the most powerful visibility asset you can build is not social media.

It is your email list.

Email remains the primary sales system for books and services alike. While social platforms fluctuate and algorithms shift without warning, an engaged email list is an owned asset. It is stable. It is direct. It is measurable.

Across industries, email marketing typically drives between 60% and 80% of direct revenue. It consistently outperforms social media in click-through rates, conversion rates, and revenue per subscriber. Average email conversion rates often range from 2% to 5% or higher, depending on the strength of the relationship and the clarity of the offer. Social media, by contrast, excels at awareness but rarely matches email in direct conversion.

This is why, inside the Blueprint, building and nurturing your email list is foundational. Not because it is trendy, but because it is reliable. It allows you to communicate directly, consistently, and strategically, without depending on platforms you do not control.

But the natural next question is: how do you grow it?

You give people a reason to join.

Case Study

Murray Eskenazi began writing novels at 88. By 90, he had published two espionage thrillers. His audience was not massive. His social media presence was minimal. By conventional standards, he didn't have a platform. But he did have something more powerful: relationships and access.

Instead of focusing on follower counts, we built a simple lead magnet—a dossier tied to his novels. It included background material, character insights, selected excerpts, and a Book Club Discussion Guide. It gave readers a reason to join his email list.

Then we identified communities already aligned with his identity and interests. Murray is deeply connected to Jewish communities, so we began outreach to Jewish ommunity centers for speaking opportunities.

Visibility did not precede the launch. It was built through it. His audience grew steadily, not explosively, but strategically.

The platform is not about volume; it is about direction.

The Fix: Build Visibility Intentionally

The fastest way to grow visibility during a launch is not to chase more followers. It is to create a simple, compelling lead magnet connected to your book.

> **For some ideas on what lead magnets you could use in your book, see Appendix B at the end of this book.**

A lead magnet does not need to be complicated. Its purpose is straightforward: exchange value for access. When someone downloads your lead magnet, they move from casual observer to connected reader. It is their first "Yes," and they step into your ecosystem. And in that moment, visibility stops being temporary and starts becoming owned.

This is how you build the asset that compounds: your email list.

From there, visibility grows through consistent communication and relational outreach. Not sporadic posting. Not algorithm chasing. Intentional communication.

This is not about going viral. It is about being deliberate. And deliberate visibility is sustainable.

Within the Blueprint, this process is strategically structured. Your book is not treated as a standalone product. It becomes the front door to a larger ecosystem. Through coaching and the Open Hours sessions, we guide you so you can design:

- A lead magnet tied directly to your book's theme
- A nurture sequence that builds trust over time
- A clear "Book → Business" backend pathway
- A re-engagement strategy for subscribers who have gone quiet

The goal is not noise. It is ownership. Books do not just need buyers; they need an audience.

Trap #5 feels like scarcity. But it is usually a lack of structure, not a lack of audience.

In the next chapter, we'll explore Trap #6—isolation and decision fatigue—and why launching alone amplifies every doubt.

"I DON'T KNOW IF I'M DOING THIS RIGHT"

There comes a point in most launches when decisions are the hardest part.

Should I change the subtitle? Is the cover strong enough? Should I lower the price? Should I send another email? Am I posting too much? Should I post more? Should I pivot?

Every choice begins to feel heavier than it should. What once felt energizing now feels draining.

Isolation and decision fatigue are real. This is Trap #6.

What This Trap Feels Like

It feels like second-guessing everything. You reread emails before sending them. You tweak the copy repeatedly. You delay publishing a post because it might not be "right." You consider asking for help, but don't want to appear unsure.

Decision fatigue sets in quietly. You wake up tired before you've even started. Small tasks feel disproportionate. And because there is no one inside the process with you, every decision feels like it carries enormous weight.

Launching a book is visible. It feels vulnerable. And vulnerability amplifies doubt. When you're alone in it, the doubt grows louder.

The root cause of this trap is not incompetence; it is cognitive overload combined with isolation.

A book launch involves dozens of decisions—pricing, timing, messaging, outreach, follow-up, and positioning. Even with a timeline, you are still choosing how to execute. And when there is no sounding board or structured space to ask questions, the brain defaults to overthinking.

Overthinking slows movement. Slowed movement increases doubt. Doubt increases isolation. It becomes a loop.

Humans are not wired to build visible things alone. We are wired for feedback.

The Hidden Cost: Burnout

The cost of isolation is rarely obvious at first. It appears as small delays. Slight hesitations. Extra days spent refining instead of releasing. But over time, those small hesitations compound. Momentum slows. Energy drops. Burnout creeps in.

And perhaps most damaging of all, you begin to internalize the pressure. You assume that if you were more confident, more decisive, more "naturally strategic," this wouldn't feel so hard.

But clarity rarely emerges in isolation. It emerges in conversation.

Case Studies

Laura, a life coach, created a book rooted in what she called her "postcard project." She mailed postcards to people in her community and invited them to write back with a question they found difficult—a question they were living with but didn't know how to answer.

The responses were beautiful, vulnerable, and profound. They became the heart of her book, *Mostly Unanswerable Questions*.

But Laura had two small children at home. Her husband worked long hospital shifts. Her time was limited, her energy divided. She could not afford endless overthinking. What kept her moving was not superhuman discipline. It was support.

She attended open hours regularly. She asked questions directly. She tested ideas out loud. She brought her social media ideas to the group for feedback. And the group supported her. She stayed in motion because she was not processing everything alone.

The book launched successfully, not because she eliminated doubt, but because she had a container strong enough to hold it. Support didn't make her dependent. It made her decisive.

Pam, a transformational guide and breathwork facilitator, didn't question the depth of her book *The Power of AND*. But when it came time to launch, a familiar doubt surfaced: Am I doing this right?

She was stepping into visibility in a new way—structuring a launch, refining her messaging, and showing up consistently. At times, she questioned whether she was doing enough… or doing it the "right" way.

Instead of getting stuck, Pam stayed inside the Blueprint.

She followed the structure, showed up for support, and brought her questions into the space rather than trying to figure everything out alone. She tested her messaging in real time, refining as she went.

The Blueprint didn't remove the question; it gave her a place to move forward with it. And that changed everything.

Instead of waiting for certainty, she stayed in motion.

Instead of striving for perfection, she focused on connection.

Pam didn't eliminate doubt; she learned how to move with it—and still launch powerfully.

The Fix: Structured Support and Accountability

The solution to this trap is not simply encouragement; it is structured support. You need a space where questions can be asked quickly and answered clearly. A place where uncertainty is normalized but stagnation is not. A place where momentum is protected.

Inside the Blueprint, this is why open hours exist. Not as a bonus. As infrastructure.

Because when authors have access to real-time feedback, decisions become lighter. When someone can bring their messaging to the call, ask for feedback, and hear, "Yes, that's strong," or "No, simplify it," movement resumes.

Accountability is not about pressure. It is about proximity.

When you are in a community of authors actively launching, motion becomes contagious. Questions that feel heavy in isolation feel solvable in community.

Support removes the illusion that you must carry every decision alone.

Trap #6 does not look dramatic; it looks like fatigue. And fatigue, left unaddressed, quietly stalls momentum.

In the next section, we'll explore the final trap—losing momentum after launch—and how to create sustainable visibility long after release week ends.

TRAP 7

"WAS THAT IT?"

Launch week arrives. You send the emails. You post the updates. You rally your launch team. You refresh the Amazon rankings. You celebrate. There is energy. There is visibility. There is applause.

And then…silence.

The emails slow. The posts become less frequent. The urgency dissolves. You wake up a few weeks later and think: *Was that it?*

Momentum Fades After the Launch is Trap #7.

What This Trap Feels Like

It feels anticlimactic. You invested months—sometimes years—into writing and publishing book. The launch felt intense, maybe even successful. But after the initial push, momentum fades faster than you expected. You may feel a subtle deflation. The book exists. It's still available, but it no longer feels alive. And you begin wondering if you missed your window.

This is one of the most common misunderstandings in publishing. Authors treat launch week as the finish line. It isn't. It's the beginning.

The root cause of this trap is the absence of a post-launch strategy. Many authors focus intensely on release week but fail to plan for what comes after. Without a defined post-launch rhythm:

- Visibility drops
- Outreach slows
- Communication becomes sporadic
- The book stops being positioned intentionally

The launch energy was temporary. But the book is not. Without structure, momentum fades naturally. Not because the book lacks value, but because attention was never designed to be sustained.

The Hidden Cost: Long-Term Visibility

The cost of this trap is long-term visibility. A book has a life cycle far longer than a week. When momentum fades prematurely:

- Speaking opportunities decline
- Email engagement decreases
- Reader referrals slow
- Revenue pathways weaken

You also lose something intangible but powerful: authority presence. Consistent visibility reinforces leadership. Sporadic visibility erodes it. The book becomes something you once launched, instead of something you continually leverage.

Case Studies

Richard Olson, a teacher and novelist, published *The Last Reprisal*, a story rooted in small-town Wisconsin life. The initial launch went well. But instead of letting momentum fade, he implemented a post-launch visibility rhythm. He scheduled speaking engagements online and in his community. He organized book signings. He continued outreach to local organizations and reading groups. He leaned into in-person visibility and community engagement.

Tia Crystal, a renowned artist, wrote *The Paintbrush*, a magical story about finding a paintbrush in Italy that changed her life forever. The book opened speaking opportunities, commissioned art pieces, group sessions, and private consulting.

Jodi Scholes, a massage therapist, wrote *The Body Blueprint: How Your Pain Tells A Story*. Her work is based on 20,000 bodies and 20+ years as a Licensed Massage Therapist. She uses her book to explain the concept of the biopsychosocial reasons for pain hiding just below the surface of our awareness. Is shoulder pain just about the shoulder? Could it be about the weight of the world on your shoulders? She even has an interactive map on her website that explains the pain associated with areas of the body. Jodi continues to use her book as a tool in speaking events.

Their books stayed active not because of constant intensity, but because of consistent positioning. Over time, that consistency built recognition. Momentum doesn't require noise. It requires continuation.

The Fix: A Post-Launch Plan and Strategic Relaunch

The solution to this trap is simple, but rarely implemented. You need a post-launch plan.

Not more intensity. More rhythm.

Most authors treat launch week as the finish line. But without a structured post-launch phase, momentum fades quickly. Inside the Blueprint, post-launch visibility is not an afterthought. It is a designed phase that sustains traction and compounds authority.

That structure includes:

- Continued email communication
- Ongoing speaking outreach
- Review and testimonial amplification
- Strategic partnerships
- Periodic visibility pushes

And the Blueprint goes a step further. It includes a fourth month of guided social media strategy specifically focused on extending visibility after launch. This phase centers on:

- Generating and showcasing reviews
- Securing speaking opportunities
- Pitching podcasts
- Guest blogging and contributed articles

Instead of disappearing after launch week, you remain visible in ways that build authority rather than exhaust it.

And perhaps most important of all: a relaunch strategy.

Every 18 to 24 months, your audience shifts. New people enter your ecosystem. Relationships deepen. Markets evolve. A relaunch is not starting over. It is reactivating momentum. The infrastructure already exists. The messaging is refined. The proof is stronger. You are not rebuilding, you are reapplying.

When you begin to view your book as a long-term platform instead of a one-time event, everything changes. The book stops being something you launched and becomes something you leverage.

This is where the authority flywheel begins.

The most successful authors do not rely on a single moment of visibility. They:

- Publish consistently
- Speak regularly
- Build and nurture their email list
- Create aligned backend offers
- Stay strategically visible

Over time, the book becomes more than a publication. It becomes a platform, a positioning tool, a lead generator, and a revenue ecosystem. Momentum compounds when rhythm replaces urgency. And when your book is treated as an asset rather than an event, it continues to work long after launch week ends.

Trap #7 is subtle. It doesn't look like failure. It looks like fading. And fading is preventable. With structure, your book continues working long after launch week ends.

THE LAUNCH SUCCESS PRINCIPLES

What Actually Makes a Book Win

By now, you've seen the traps. You understand how launches stall quietly, how momentum fades, how overwhelm and isolation and lack of structure can undermine even strong books. But avoiding traps is only half the equation. Sustainable launch success is built on principles.

Over three decades of publishing and launching books, I've watched patterns repeat. Platforms evolve. Technology accelerates. Marketing tactics change. But certain truths remain constant. When authors anchor themselves in these truths, their launches become grounded instead of reactive. Their books stop feeling fragile. Their momentum becomes durable.

The first principle is simple and powerful: correct and continue.

I do not believe in failed launches. I believe in data. If visibility was low, that's data. If monetization wasn't clear, that's data. If momentum faded, that's data. Many authors treat imperfect results as personal failure. They internalize it and retreat. Successful authors do something different. They adjust. They refine. They relaunch strategically. The difference between books that grow and books that stall is not perfection. It is persistence guided by feedback. Correction is strength. Continuation is strategy.

Closely connected to this is the principle of momentum over perfection. Perfection stalls. Momentum compounds. You can tweak a landing page for weeks. You can rewrite an email ten times. You can delay outreach until everything feels polished and safe. Or you can move. Momentum builds clarity faster than contemplation ever will. A slightly imperfect message sent consistently will outperform a perfect message sent too late. Launches thrive on movement. And movement builds confidence.

Underneath all of this sits something deeper: your book's purpose matters.

Your book did not come through you randomly. It carries intention. Whether it is meant to shift thinking, solve a problem, elevate awareness, entertain, or transform, it exists for a reason. When you remember that, marketing stops feeling self-promotional. It becomes stewardship. You are not pushing a product. You are positioning a message. Authors who remain anchored in purpose outlast discouragement because they are not chasing applause. They are honoring impact.

Another principle that cannot be overstated is this: stages are a force multiplier. Speaking, whether in person or virtual, accelerates authority and trust faster than almost any other channel. Live audiences convert at dramatically higher rates than passive exposure. One well-positioned speaking opportunity can outperform weeks of scattered posting. On a stage, you are not just selling a book; you are activating a room. Over time, speaking compounds visibility and credibility in a way that few tactics can replicate. Your book gives you a reason to be on stages. Use it.

Launch success is also relational. Books spread through people, not algorithms. The strongest launches I have witnessed were not built on flashy tactics but on real relationships. Launch teams, endorsements, partnerships, reader engagement—these are not accessories. They are infrastructure. When supporters feel included in the mission of your message, they share it. When readers feel seen, they advocate. When relationships are nurtured, momentum builds. Authors who win in the long term treat their audience like a community, not a metric.

And at the center of it all sits one of the most practical truths in publishing: your email list is your primary sales system. Social media creates visibility. Email builds relationships. Platforms fluctuate. Algorithms change. Reach shifts. But your email list is owned, direct, measurable, and stable. Most direct book sales and service conversions happen through email, not posts. An engaged list, even a modest one, will outperform a large disengaged following every time. If you build nothing else strategically, build this.

When you integrate these principles—correct and continue, momentum over perfection, purpose over ego, stages as multipliers, relationships over algorithms, email as foundation—you no longer launch reactively. You launch strategically. And strategy creates freedom. Freedom from guessing. Freedom from comparison. Freedom from burnout.

This is why the Blueprint is structured the way it is. Not to give you more to do, but to give you clarity about what matters. It integrates every principle you've just read. It provides structure so you can move with momentum. It anchors you in purpose. It builds your email system. It activates stages. It strengthens relationships. It turns correction into iteration instead of retreat.

Launch success is not accidental. It is designed. And design creates durability.

Your book deserves durability.

And so does your business.

YOUR BOOK HAS A PURPOSE

At some point—before there was a manuscript, before there was a title, before there was a table of contents—there was a knowing.

A pull. A persistence. An idea that would not leave you alone.

You honored that knowing once when you wrote your book. Now you are being invited to honor it again.

Because books do not exist merely to be written, they exist to travel. They exist to reach the people they were meant to reach. They exist to shape conversations, shift thinking, build bridges, open doors, and create pathways.

If your book is meant to grow your business, then launching it strategically is not self-promotion. It is stewardship. It is the conscious positioning of something that carries purpose.

You have seen the traps. You understand what stalls momentum. You know now that launches rarely fail loudly— they drift quietly. They stall in hesitation. They fade in isolation. They weaken without structure.

But drifting does not have to be your story.

Your book is not here by accident. And neither are you.

So this is the moment where intention becomes commitment.

You can choose to honor your book's purpose—not casually, but deliberately. You can choose to treat it not as a product, but as a platform. You can choose to position it with clarity and integrity instead of waiting for perfect conditions.

You can release perfection. You can release hesitation. You can release the need for applause before action.

And you can choose momentum. You can choose impact.

If you have launched before and felt disappointed, correct and continue. What happened was data, not defeat. Adjust. Refine. Relaunch with structure.

If you have not launched yet, begin. Set the date. Build the framework. Invite the people.

If momentum has faded, remember that books are not one-week events. Every eighteen to twenty-four months, your audience shifts. New people enter your ecosystem. Relationships deepen. Markets evolve. Your authority expands. A relaunch is not starting over—it is reactivating what already exists.

Your book is not finished because launch week passed. It is activated every time you position it intentionally.

Keep going.

Keep refining.

Keep showing up.

Let your book travel. Let it build relationships. Let it open stages. Let it generate opportunities. Let it serve.

Because your book did not come through you to sit quietly, it came to move.

And when you honor both births—the birth of creation and the birth of impact—you fulfill the agreement you made not just with your business, but with the message itself.

Now let your book do what it was born to do.

THE 90-DAY BOOK LAUNCH BLUEPRINT

The Blueprint is designed for you—the author who wants to become a best seller, share your message with the world, and grow your business. But you have no idea where to begin, how to launch, or even if you're doing it the right way.

Book launching, marketing, and promotion may not seem simple at first, but they can be. The 90-Day Book Launch Blueprint can show you how.

The Blueprint is a proven, step-by-step system designed to help authors successfully launch—or relaunch—their books with confidence, clarity, and impact. Whether your book is freshly written or already published, this program guides you through every stage of the launch process, from aligning your message with your business to building a launch team, creating compelling content, and generating buzz across media and social platforms. With templates, timelines, and expert support, you'll avoid common mistakes, amplify your reach, and turn your book into a powerful tool for growth, visibility, and income.

As you've seen in this book, the Blueprint solves seven significant problems that authors face every day:

- What to do when
- Overwhelm
- How to make a profit
- No marketing expertise
- Lack of visibility
- Isolation and decision fatigue
- Uncertainty about post-launch

The 7 Problems the Blueprint Solves

1. EcoSystem Strategy | "I don't know how to turn my book into income."

    → You'll receive a clear ecosystem strategy and revenue plan designed to generate $10K+ from your book.

2. Amazon Bestseller Strategy | "I want credibility, but don't know how to get there."

    → You'll follow a proven Amazon Bestseller strategy to elevate your authority and visibility.

3. Tech Intimidation | "I'm not tech-savvy and don't know how to set all of this up."

    → You'll get step-by-step guidance, templates, and tools that simplify the tech—so you can execute without confusion or frustration.

4. No Visibility Systems | "I don't have a system to consistently get seen or attract readers."

    → You'll implement clear visibility and marketing systems that position your book in front of the right audience—before, during, and after your launch.

5. Overwhelm | "I feel overwhelmed and don't know what to do first."

    → A customized 90-day timeline shows you exactly what to do—week by week.

6. Community | "I'm doing this alone."

    → You'll be supported by a community of authors launching alongside you.

7. Post-Launch Strategy | "Was that it? I don't want this to be a one-time launch."

    → You'll have lifetime access so you can relaunch and scale again and again.

For those who don't have the bandwidth to launch their book, we also offer private coaching and done-for-you services. Prices are based on the type of support you need. We are committed to your success.

What's Included

- **Lifetime Access to the 90-Day Book Launch Blueprint**

  Self-guided course curriculum with 24/7 access, you can launch your next book or relaunch one that's been on the market a while.

- **Customized Timeline**

  A timeline of every step in your book launch customized with your launch date, so you know what to do and when to do it, so you can stay on track. The timeline helps eliminate stress during your launch.

- **Strategic Plan on how you can make a Profit**

  A custom plan where you can calculate how to make your launch profitable in book sales, book signing parties, speaking gigs, collaborations, and new clients.

- **3-Month Social Media Marketing Strategy**

  A comprehensive marketing and social media strategy with 60 posts, including content, graphic templates, and when to post.

- **Email Templates Ready to Send**

  A customizable series of prewritten email templates to send to your Launch Team, to get endorsements for your book, to be a guest on podcasts, and to get professional book reviews.

- **Media Kit Template**

  A customizable template to build a valuable media kit and press release you can use to get you, your book, and your business into the eye of the media.

- **Book Trailer Video Template**

  Instructions and examples of great book trailer videos to help you create an awesome, attention-grabbing trailer for your book.

- **Lead Magnets From Your Book Content**

  Creating a lead magnet from some content in your book to build your mailing list.

- **Website Landing Page Template for Your Book**

  A guide to know what to put where on your website page and your book launch team pages.

- **Book Signing Party Guide**

  A template on how to host a live book signing party, what to include at the event, and more.

- **Lists of Podcasts, Book Promotion Sites, Literary Awards, Professional Reviewers, and Guest Blog Sites**

  Access to a valuable resource of podcasts and literary awards that you can use to promote your book.

- **Accountability & Support**

  Weekly Open Hours Live Support on Zoom. Email reminders to keep you on track during your 90-day launch. Private coaching is also available to support and streamline your book marketing efforts.

The Blueprint will guide you on these topics and more:

- Your Timeline
- Strategic Forecasting to $10K+
- 100 Marketing Strategy
- Email Campaigns
- Amazon Bestseller Campaign
- Website Landing Pages
- Lead Magnets
- Book Trailer Videos
- Author Pages
- Social Media Content Creation
- Book Launch Party
- Optimizing Social Media

- Book Metadata
- Blog Writing & Guest Blogging
- Speaking Gigs
- Building Your Launch Team
- Launch Team Prizes
- Endorsements
- Professional Reviews
- Literary Awards
- Podcasts
- Media Kit & Press Release
- Book Promotion Sites
- How to Get Your Book in Bookstores
- Amazon Author Page

Click here to learn more and enroll in the 90-Day Book Launch Blueprint: https://quantumshiftmedia. com/90-day-book-launch

LAUNCH SELF-ASSESSMENT

Before you relaunch—or before you launch at all—pause and assess where you are. Answer each question honestly:

Clarity

- Do I have a defined launch date?
- Do I know exactly who this book is for?
- Can I clearly articulate what transformation it creates?
- Is there a visible next step after someone finishes reading?

Visibility

- Do I have an email list?
- Do I communicate with it consistently?
- Do I have at least one primary visibility channel chosen?
- Do I have a lead magnet connected to this book?

Integration

- Does my book clearly connect to my business offers?
- Is there a defined revenue pathway beyond book sales?
- Have I structured speaking, consulting, or programs around it?

Momentum

- Do I have a post-launch plan?
- Have I identified review amplification strategies?
- Do I have a relaunch plan for the future?

If you answered "no" to more than three of these, your launch likely lacks structure—not effort. That is a design issue, not a talent issue. The 90-Day Book Launch Blueprint can help you resolve these critical issues. And when you come to the Book Launch Open Hours, we can guide you on how you can use your book to grow your business.

LEAD MAGNET IDEAS CONNECTED TO FICTION & NONFICTION BOOKS

A lead magnet should extend your book—not distract from it. Every book needs a lead magnet embedded in it to connect with your readers. The best lead magnet is not necessarily the most elaborate—it is the one most closely connected to the reader's experience of your book.

Here are some lead magnet ideas:

1. A downloadable checklist from one chapter
2. A "Quick Start" implementation guide
3. A companion workbook
4. A case study expansion
5. A bonus chapter
6. An audio teaching on one core concept
7. A private podcast series
8. A live training replay
9. A free assessment or quiz
10. A curated resource list

11. A template or script from the book

12. A behind-the-scenes story not included in the book

13. A "Top 10 Mistakes" cheat sheet

14. A 5-day email mini-course

15. A research summary or data breakdown

16. A printable action planner

17. A video walkthrough of your framework

18. A sample chapter from your next book

19. A diagnostic tool

20. A free strategy call application (selectively offered)

21. A private reader community or discussion group

22. A book club discussion guide

23. A guided reflection journal based on the book

24. A downloadable framework diagram or visual map

25. A "Start Here" roadmap for applying the book

26. A scorecard to measure progress on the book's principles

27. A swipe file of examples referenced in the book

28. A decision-making flowchart related to the topic

29. A printable worksheet for a key exercise

30. A companion slide deck summarizing the core framework

31. A glossary of key concepts used in the book

32. A personal story archive or extended narrative scenes

33. A guided meditation or reflection tied to the book's theme

34. A monthly implementation challenge

35. A curated reading list for deeper study

36. A short email course expanding one chapter

37. A "tools and apps" guide that supports the book's ideas

38. A fill-in-the-blank planning template

39. A habit tracker aligned with the book's methodology

40. A video interview with an expert mentioned in the book

41. A private Q&A session for readers

42. A downloadable infographic summarizing the framework

43. A "next steps" roadmap for advanced readers

44. A reader feedback survey with bonus insights

45. A certification pathway or deeper training opportunity

For nonfiction authors—especially those using a book to grow a business—some lead magnets consistently outperform others because they move readers quickly from insight to action. These are the ones that most reliably convert readers into subscribers, clients, or community members.

The 10 Highest-Converting Lead Magnets for Nonfiction Authors

1. The Quick-Start Implementation Guide

A short guide that shows readers exactly how to apply the core framework from your book in the first 24–48 hours. Readers love immediate progress, and this removes the overwhelm of figuring out where to begin.

2. The Self-Assessment or Diagnostic Quiz

People love discovering where they stand. A well-designed assessment helps readers evaluate their current situation and see exactly how your framework applies to them.

3. A Companion Workbook

A workbook transforms passive reading into active implementation. When readers write, reflect, and work through exercises, they become more invested in your ideas—and in you.

4. A Chapter Expansion or Bonus Chapter

This works well when a chapter introduces a concept but cannot explore it fully in the book. The bonus material deepens the reader's understanding and reinforces your expertise.

5. A "Top Mistakes" or "Hidden Traps" Cheat Sheet

People are highly motivated to avoid mistakes. A concise cheat sheet that highlights the most common pitfalls in your topic often gets strong opt-in rates.

6. Templates, Scripts, or Swipe Files

Readers appreciate tools they can immediately use. Templates, email scripts, outlines, and planning frameworks are extremely practical and highly valued.

7. A Short Email Mini-Course

A 5–7 day email series allows you to guide readers step-by-step through a concept from the book. It builds trust while introducing them to your ecosystem.

8. A Private Podcast or Audio Teaching Series

Audio content allows readers to deepen their learning while commuting, walking, or exercising. It also strengthens the personal connection to you as the author.

9. A Case Study Library

Readers love seeing how ideas work in real life. Expanding the book with real-world examples of people who successfully applied the framework builds credibility.

10. A Reader Community or Discussion Group

This transforms a one-time reader into a long-term participant in your ecosystem. It also creates peer reinforcement around the ideas in your book.

Lead Magnet Ideas for Fiction Authors

Lead magnets work just as effectively for fiction authors as they do for nonfiction authors—but the purpose is different.

Nonfiction lead magnets typically help readers apply the ideas or frameworks presented in the book. Fiction lead magnets, on the other hand, extend the experience of the story itself. They draw readers deeper into the characters, the world, and the imagination behind it.

Instead of teaching a process, fiction lead magnets deepen the reader's connection to the story world and build anticipation for future books. When done well, they make readers feel like insiders in the author's universe. And when readers become emotionally invested in the characters and the world of the story, they are far more likely to follow the author from one book to the next.

The Goal for Fiction Authors

The best fiction lead magnets typically do one of three things:

- Expand the story world
- Deepen the reader's emotional connection to the characters
- Build anticipation for the next book

When designed intentionally, a lead magnet can transform a casual reader into a loyal fan who eagerly follows the author from book to book.

Here are some lead magnet ideas fiction authors can use:

A prequel short story
A story that takes place before the events of the book, revealing how a character became who they are.

A bonus epilogue or additional scene
An extra scene that continues the story beyond the ending of the book.

A deleted scene
A scene that didn't make the final version of the book but adds insight into the characters or plot.

A character backstory

A deeper look into the history, motivations, or past experiences of a major character.

A side-character short story

A story told from the perspective of a supporting character.

An alternate point-of-view scene

A key moment from the book retold from another character's perspective.

A world-building guide

A short guide explaining the setting, culture, or rules of the story world.

A map of the story world

Especially powerful for fantasy, historical fiction, and adventure novels.

A timeline of events

A visual timeline showing important events in the story universe.

A character guide

Profiles of the main characters and their relationships.

A book club discussion guide

Questions designed to help readers explore the themes and motivations in the story.

A "Which Character Are You?" quiz

An engaging way for readers to connect with the characters.

Research notes or inspiration behind the story
Insights into what inspired the book or the research behind it.

A playlist inspired by the book
Music that shaped the tone or writing process.

The first chapter of the next book in the series
A powerful way to build anticipation for the next installment.

A bridge story between books in a series
A short story that fills the gap between two novels.

An audiobook sample or narrated short story
Allows readers to experience the author's storytelling in audio form.

For fiction authors, the highest-converting lead magnets share one important trait: **they give readers more of what they already loved about the book**. Instead of teaching, they deepen the story experience and strengthen emotional attachment to the characters and world.

The 10 Highest-Converting Lead Magnets for Fiction Authors

Here are the 10 lead magnets that consistently convert the best for fiction authors.

1. A Prequel Short Story

This is one of the most effective lead magnets in fiction. A prequel reveals events that happened before the book and shows readers how a character became who they are. It feels like a secret piece of the story world readers wouldn't want to miss.

2. A Bonus Epilogue or Additional Scene

Readers often want to know what happens next. A bonus epilogue gives them closure—or a hint of what's coming in the next book. This works particularly well at the end of a novel.

3. The First Chapter of the Next Book

Nothing drives subscriptions like curiosity. Offering the opening chapter of the next book in a series creates anticipation and encourages readers to stay connected.

4. A Bridge Story Between Books

A short story that takes place between two novels helps keep readers engaged while they wait for the next installment. Many bestselling series authors use this technique.

5. A Character Backstory or Origin Story

Readers love discovering hidden details about characters. A short story explaining a character's past or motivations can deepen emotional investment in the series.

6. A Deleted Scene

Scenes that didn't make the final version of the book can still be fascinating to readers. They provide a behind-the-curtain glimpse into the story.

7. A "Meet the Characters" Guide

A visual or narrative guide introducing the main characters, their motivations, and their relationships helps readers connect more deeply with the story. This works particularly well for fantasy, romance, and ensemble casts.

8. A Map or World Guide

For fantasy, historical fiction, and adventure stories, readers love exploring the world of the book. A downloadable map or guide can make the story universe feel more real.

9. A Book Club Discussion Guide

Many fiction readers participate in book clubs. Providing discussion questions helps book clubs choose and explore the book more deeply. It also encourages group discovery of the author.

10. A "Which Character Are You?" Quiz

Interactive content performs extremely well. A personality quiz tied to the story's characters engages readers and encourages sharing. It also introduces readers to the characters in a fun way.

The Key Principle

The best fiction lead magnets do one of three things:

- Expand the story world
- Deepen emotional connection to characters
- Build anticipation for the next book

When a lead magnet accomplishes one of these goals, it turns a one-time reader into a loyal fan who follows the author from book to book.

There are many more lead magnets you could create. The key is not complexity—it is alignment. The best lead magnets deepen the reader's engagement with the ideas in your book and help them begin applying what they have learned.

The most effective lead magnets are not random bonuses. They are the next step in the reader's journey.

Your book provides the insight. Your lead magnet provides the implementation.

Together, they form a simple bridge—moving the reader from book buyer to ecosystem participant.

Your book opens the door. Your lead magnet begins the relationship.

When designed intentionally, this bridge turns readers into subscribers, participants, clients, and advocates for your work.

About QR Codes

Many authors now include a QR code alongside the link so readers can quickly access the lead magnet on their phones. I used them several times in this book.

Where to Place Your Lead Magnet

Many authors don't realize where the lead magnet should appear in the book.

Your lead magnet should appear in at least two places in your book:

- At the front of the book, shortly after the table of contents.
- At the end of the book, when the reader has finished the story.

Readers who enjoy your book are most likely to join your list immediately after finishing it, when their emotional connection is strongest. Make the invitation simple and clear, with a direct link or QR code.

A book without a lead magnet is a missed opportunity. Readers may love your work, but without a clear next step, most will simply close the book and move on. A well-designed lead magnet keeps the conversation going and allows the relationship with the reader to continue long after the final page.

SIMPLE "BOOK-TO-BUSINESS" PATHWAY MAP

Your book should not exist in isolation. Here are a few simple pathway models:

Option 1: Book → Lead Magnet → Email Nurture → Offer

Option 2: Book → Downloadable Resource → Email Relationship → Speaking Invitation or Program Enrollment

Option 3: Book → Assessment Tool → Consultation → High-Ticket Offer

If you cannot draw your pathway on one page, it likely needs refinement. Keep in mind clarity before visibility.

POST-LAUNCH MOMENTUM CHECKLIST

Launch week is the beginning, not the end. Use this checklist after your launch:

- Send follow-up email recap
- Highlight reviews publicly on your website and social media
- Pitch 10 podcast hosts and get booked for one podcast per week
- Reach out to 5 speaking venues and book a speaking gig
- Post 3 testimonial graphics
- Invite readers to share photos of the book
- Revisit your lead magnet positioning and how it is responding
- Evaluate conversion metrics
- Schedule another visibility push for 90 days out
- Mark calendar for 18–24 month relaunch

And use the 90-Day Book Launch Blueprint again, including all the content you wrote and created. You don't have to rethink it all over again, reuse it, and relaunch it. Momentum is maintained by rhythm, not intensity.

ABOUT THE AUTHOR

At Quantum Shift Media, Keren Kilgore helps authors, coaches, speakers, and business owners write, publish, and market fiction and nonfiction books that align with their deepest truth and professional purpose—transforming them into powerful business assets that grow visibility, impact, and income. With more than 30 years of experience in publishing, she guides clients through every phase of the process—from crafting a compelling manuscript to designing the book and implementing a strategic launch that attracts clients, speaking engagements, and media attention. Her services include book coaching, publishing, design, author branding, and marketing campaigns, including her signature 90-Day Book Launch Blueprint.

Keren is known not only for her editorial insight but for her ability to help authors architect platforms. She believes a book is not just a product—it is a platform and a portal into the work you are here to do in the world. Her passion is helping authors activate their authority and position their books as long-term assets that create both transformation and revenue.

A certified Mastery of Self Facilitator trained in the Transformational Meditation™ Model developed by the International Academy of Self-Knowledge, Keren also guides individuals through the Mastery of Self Intensive, a powerful process designed to help people release limiting patterns, reconnect with their Higher Power, and step into authentic freedom—all in 28 days. At her core, Keren believes transformation is not about becoming more, it's about the law of subtraction—releasing what you are not.

Beyond her professional life, Keren's story is one of adventure, commitment, and deep love. She and her husband, Michael, were foster parents to 26 teenagers over nine years, opening their home and hearts to young lives in transition. They have lived in beautiful places across the United States and in Kampala, Uganda, gathering community and perspective wherever they've gone.

For many years, Keren and Michael rode BMW motorcycles across North America—from California to Key West, from the Canadian ice fields to Mexico—and even completed an Iron Butt ride, traveling 1,000 miles in 24 hours. They are the proud parents of two children and grandparents to four grandchildren who light up their world.

Now living in Florida and celebrating 45 years together, Keren and Michael focus on true fun—paddleboarding, beach time, traveling, pickleball Tuesdays, game nights, building community, and creating effervescent collaborations that bring people together.

Keren can be reached at Keren@QuantumShiftMedia.com.

To learn more about the 90-Day Book Launch Blueprint and additional resources for authors, visit: https://QuantumShiftMedia.com

WORK WITH QUANTUM SHIFT MEDIA

At Quantum Shift Media, we help authors write, publish, and market books that grow businesses. We also publish fiction work, children's books, and young adult books. With all of our books, authors retain all rights and revenues. Our services include:

Professional Strategic Book-to-Business Assessment

Author Coaching, Editing, Strategic Book Positioning

Editing Ghostwriting- Developmental and Substantial

Hybrid Publishing

Professional Cover Design

Professional Interior Design

90-Day Book Launch Blueprint

Book Marketing Done-For-You

Book-To-Business Strategy Sessions

Branding

Website EcoSystem

Flow Writing Workshops

Visit QuantumShiftMedia.com for more information and free resources that support authors.

To see how these strategies have helped other authors, visit our testimonials page where clients share their experiences working with us:

https://quantumshiftmedia.com/testimonies

Their stories reflect the level of care, expertise, and results we strive to provide every author we work with.

If you're ready to turn your book into a platform that attracts readers, opportunities, and clients, you can learn more about the **90-Day Book Launch Blueprint** and additional author resources at:

https://quantumshiftmedia.com